Paul Anderton and Robin Daly
of Two Dirty Boys

REGROWN

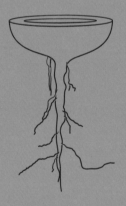

How to Grow Fruit, Herbs and Vegetables
from Kitchen Scraps

Hardie Grant

BOOKS

REGROWN

How to Grow Fruit, Herbs and Vegetables from Kitchen Scraps

Contents

Introduction

There are many magical things in life that are easy to take for granted, like a brilliant blue sky or the changing of the seasons. All you have to do is spend a moment contemplating these things and you are likely to feel a sense of awe and wonder.

Like something from a science fiction novel, plants have an extraordinary ability to reproduce themselves without fertilisation. Even your everyday kitchen scraps carry in their cells all the messaging they need to generate countless new versions of themselves. In its simplest form, a small living section of a scrap can be watered and nurtured into a fully revitalised version of its former self. We call this propagation, and it's mind-bending.

This book will show you how to turn your kitchen waste into edible or ornamental new vegetables, fruits, herbs and plants. We will explain, with simple step-by-step instructions, how to breathe fresh life into your cuttings or germinate dormant fruit seeds which were bound for your waste bin.

There are so many reasons to try regrowing your own scraps. Here are just a few.

It's energising and rewarding

Some cuttings visibly show new growth within hours. From that point onwards, you'll see daily changes to your cuttings. Roots emerge, small green shoots come to life from nowhere and revived crops begin to take on new shapes. There are few things more rewarding than knowing you've played a part in something so awe-inspiring.

It's cost-effective

Regrowing scraps and cuttings can reward you with fresh homegrown food which can help reduce your grocery bill. If your shopping habits are anything like ours, you can be caught out when popping down to a local store to grab just a couple of key ingredients, only to return home with far more than you budgeted for. Having a supply of fresh produce growing on your windowsills might mean you won't have to make the trip in the first place – you won't even need to put your shoes on to harvest the greens for a fresh summer salad.

They look great

The trend for houseplants has seen their monetary value increase in recent years, particularly in urban settings. Many of us have come to appreciate living amongst greenery, not just for the health benefits (including an increased oxygen supply and better sleeping habits), but also for the peaceful and tranquil aesthetic that a room full of plants creates. Growing vegetables in glass containers or in pots of your choice gives you an opportunity to fill your home with new life and positive energy. The winding new roots of an avocado seed in a glass of water have an eye-catching graphic quality when caught in a shaft of light on your windowsill, while the green shoots of root ginger resemble a miniature indoor bamboo plant.

It's good for the environment (and for you)

When you regrow from kitchen scraps, you're essentially recycling waste. By drawing extra life from your cuttings, you're helping to reduce carbon emissions by eliminating the need for producers somewhere else in the world to grow your lunch, package it and transport it to your supermarket. You could think of your journey into regrowing as a nod to self-sufficiency. But it's worth noting that you probably won't be able to give up the supermarket quite yet, unless you have acres of windowsills in your home.

It's a great way to learn

If you're new to gardening or growing your own, the task ahead can feel like a minefield of dos and don'ts. A visit to a garden centre or plant nursery can be costly, and not everybody has the space to haphazardly learn by experience, as we have, in allotments (community gardens) or large gardens. So, regrowing your kitchen scraps is a wonderful way to learn and find inspiration in nature without a huge investment (both in time and money). As you progress, you'll become more and more familiar with what different types of plants need and how to make adjustments to their environments to enhance growth and vitality. Once you've mastered regrowing at home, the sky's the limit.

Key elements for success

Flowering regrown leeks

You

It might sound daunting if you're new to gardening, but the most important element if you are to grow things successfully at home is you. As you embark on your regrowing projects, you will learn to watch and listen carefully to your growing harvest. The plants' behaviour and state of health will be clear to see. The cuttings themselves will warn you if their environment is too hot, too cold or too dry, or if they are in need of some fresh water.

Light

All plants need a different intensity of light and darkness depending on where in the world they originally come from and the conditions of their natural habitat. A bright window will provide enough light for most of the projects in this book; however, if you live in a particularly dark environment or you're planning to regrow over the darker months, you might choose to invest in an artificial grow light.

Temperature

Each plant has its own optimal temperature for growth. For each of the projects in this book, we've provided a guide to show whether the cutting prefers warmer or cooler conditions. Not everyone has the luxury of being able to alter the temperature of different zones in their home on command, so our notes on temperature are a general rule of thumb, but it would be wise to pick items to regrow based on the conditions available to you at home.

Soil

Although the majority of the projects outlined in this book start off growing in water, you will get the most out of these fruits and vegetables if you transplant them into soil as they mature. The soil contains the food your plants will need to grow strong. It's best to use a soilless mix if you're growing plants indoors. Some gardeners also choose to sterilise soil in advance to avoid bacterial or fungal infections later on in the growing process. It might sound crazy, but this can be done at home by 'cooking' the soil on a baking tray in your oven for 30 minutes at 200°C (180°C fan/400°F/gas 6).

Containers

We've suggested a container type for each regrowing project, but these are just ideas. Personally, we get a kick out of reusing glass and plastic containers which were bound for the garbage or recycling bins. Depending on the required size and shape, you can use yogurt pots, jam jars, drinking glasses, ice cream tubs, ready-meal trays, plastic milk cartons and so on. In fact, anything you can lay your hands on will work, providing it's a suitable shape and you can make drainage holes (if required) in the bottom.

Water

Although this can be quite frustrating for people who are new to gardening, there's no hard and fast rule as to how often you should water your plants, or how much water you should give them. It varies, depending on the humidity and temperature of your home. However, you don't have to be a genius to become familiar with how moist soil should look and feel. It's neither dry nor soaking wet, but a happy in-between. Because of this need, adequate drainage is really important when it comes to achieving a healthy plant.

Humidity

You can simulate moisture in the air with the use of a spray bottle or mister filled with water. Celery, for example, requires a daily spritz to stop it from drying out, as do mushrooms. Plastic or cling film (plastic wrap) is another way to control humidity by simulating a mini greenhouse. You'll see this technique used with tomatoes later on.

Seasons

The time of year can be important to your project. Most varieties of potatoes, for instance, are best planted at the beginning of spring, and some plants that require lots of sunlight might fare better over the summer months. Luckily in our modern homes, we can create a temperate climate all year long, but the quality and health of the starter plant also plays a role in regrowing vegetables and fruit, so try to start your projects when your chosen mother plant is in season.

Rot

The conditions we strive to create to encourage our cuttings to regrow are also the perfect starter homes for a range of unwanted impostors. Rot, fungus and bacteria are common threats when you regrow your fruit and vegetables. Ensure your cuttings are clean and healthy to start off with. Potted plants must have adequate drainage. When it comes to cuttings standing in water, make sure you regularly refresh the liquid, even if it seems perfectly clean and clear – this is crucial in fighting off rot. You'll know something has taken a bad turn if the plant starts to produce an unpleasant odour, becomes slimy or shows signs of mould spots. To avoid this, it's a good idea to refresh the water first thing in the morning as part of your daily routine. This makes for a rewarding start to each day as you take stock of your harvest and observe small, but certain, changes to your growing crop.

Bugs

If you choose to transfer some of your regrowing projects to the outdoors, whether to a plant pot on a balcony, or to a garden or allotment (community garden), you'll also expose your cuttings to unwanted insects. Aphids often bother our crops on the allotment, and we've worked out a safe and organic way to repel them by adding fresh, finely chopped garlic to spray bottles of water and spritzing the affected plants. Besides this, there are many products on the market to help with an infestation, but often the best thing to do is squash these bothersome little flies with your fingers. It's gross, but it works.

Quantity

When we first started the process of regrowing, we did so in such small quantities that the cuttings generated just about enough food for Barbie's brunch. However, if you get into the habit of continually saving potential plants before they get to your compost bin, you'll find you are rewarded with a decent-sized harvest when the time comes. If you want to increase your yield, consider using plastic trays to regrow multiple cuttings side by side. Why not take regrowing to an industrial scale if you have the space? You might be surprised at quite how self-sufficient you could be.

Regrown

High-speed growers

Spring onions

(Scallions)

Spring onions (scallions) really are a great place to start if you're new to caring for plants or gardening. By following a few simple steps, you'll be rewarded for your efforts within days.

If you enjoy cooking a variety of dishes, you're probably used to working with spring onions. Their mild but distinctive flavour means they can be used in fresh dishes and salads or cooked in stir-fries. They're also perfect for those last-minute improvised creations. Try pickling regrown spring onions with mustard seeds, fennel seeds and chilli flakes (hot red pepper flakes) – this makes a perfect gift for your host at a summer barbecue.

It's best to use the freshest products you can find if you're planning to regrow your scraps. We like to keep multiple spring onion cuttings growing at the same time – think of it as your own indoor vegetable patch. Just harvest as and when you need them.

Spring onions offer a stronger taste if regrown in pots of potting compost (peat-free). If you'd like to take this extra step, a bright but cool spot (either indoors out outdoors) will be ideal for your pot.

Growing speed	Fast
Difficulty level	Easy
Position	Partial sun/sunny
Temperature	Cool
Use	Edible
Container	Small/medium/large

You will need

Scissors or sharp knife
Jam jar or drinking glass
Pebbles or marbles
Fresh water and a sunny spot
Potting compost (optional)
Plant pot with drainage holes and drip tray (optional)

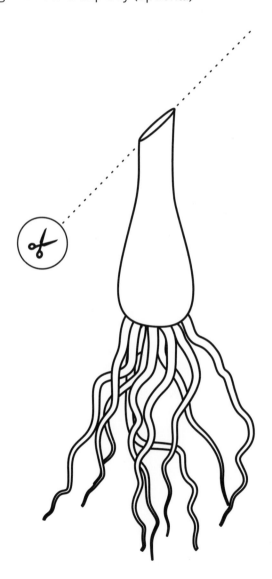

To regrow spring onion scraps

1   Using kitchen scissors or a sharp knife, cut the bottom 2.5–5cm (1–2in) off the spring onions. You're aiming to retain the roots and two-thirds of the white bulbous area, so your plant can start regrowing immediately.

2   Your choice of glass jar or drinking glass will depend on how many spring onions you're growing at any one time. Fill the jar or glass with pebbles or marbles to a depth of about 2.5cm (1in). These will stabilise your spring onions as they grow.

3   Now gently insert the spring onions amongst the pebbles. Add enough cool fresh water to reach just above the roots of your cuttings.

4   Place the jar in a sunny but cool environment. A bright kitchen windowsill would be ideal.

5 Each morning, you'll need to drain and refresh the jar with new water. It only takes a moment, but it's critical to keep your crop fresh. If your crop is feeling a little greasy to the touch, or the water is smelling strongly of onion, you'll need to increase the frequency at which you refresh your water.

6 Within the first 24–48 hours, you will notice that your perfectly sliced onion tops are starting to change shape. Green shoots will emerge from the tops of the cuttings, and within a couple of weeks your spring onion greens will be miraculously renewed and ready to be used in the kitchen.

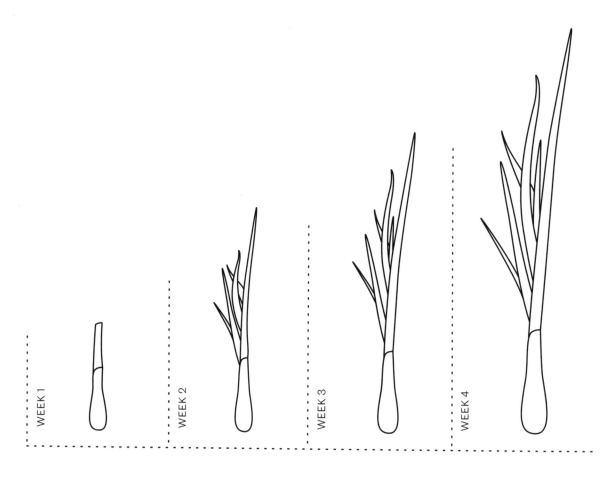

WEEK 1 WEEK 2 WEEK 3 WEEK 4

Tips

○ Consider regrowing a larger number of spring onion cuttings to increase the yield.

○ If your spring onions develop any signs of rot, try removing the outer layer of skin and refreshing the water a little more frequently.

○ When trimming back the spring onions, avoid cutting too close to the white bulbous base, as this can inhibit the plant's regrowth.

○ Spring onions can be regrown three or four times before they lose their magic.

Regrown

Bean sprouts

If you like the idea of a fast-turnaround crop, consider sprouting your own mung beans, alfalfa or lentils. Overall the process is pretty straightforward, as you'll simply be providing fresh water and drainage, but good hygiene and regular attention are really important with this project. You'll be tending to your little bean babies a few times a day until they're ready to be eaten.

It's also important that you use untreated, and most of all clean seeds. Do consider purchasing your initial seeds from retailers specialising in seeds for sprouting at home. When you kickstart the sprouting process, you'll also be creating the perfect environment for unwanted bacteria, so follow the steps closely to make sure your home harvest is fit for purpose.

Growing speed	Fast
Difficulty level	Easy
Position	Shady
Temperature	Cool
Use	Edible
Container	Small

You will need

Sieve (strainer)
Jam jar
Fresh water
Tea towel (dish towel)
Elastic band
Small plate, saucer or bowl

To regrow bean sprouts

1   Start by rinsing your beans or seeds in a sieve (strainer) and removing any imperfect specimens. Make sure they are clean and that there are no unwanted pieces of organic matter in the mix that might contaminate your harvest.

2   Take a freshly cleaned jam jar and place your beans or seeds inside. They should only take up around a quarter of the space in the jar (or a little less than this if you're growing alfalfa). Once the beans have sprouted, they will magically expand and fill the remaining space, so this is crucial.

3   Fill the jar with fresh, cool water and cover with a clean tea towel (dish towel), secured in place around the top of the jar with an elastic band. This covering will allow you to water the beans, but also you can drain them easily so they aren't left in standing water.

4   Leave the beans or seeds to soak for around 12 hours in a cool location away from direct sunlight.

5   Now you need to drain away the water and rinse your crop. Once you have done this, replace the tea-towel lid, but this time position the jar upside down and at a slight angle. This will allow any excess water to drain off, while still allowing air to circulate in your jar. You might want to do this over a plate or small bowl to catch the water.

6   Here's the part where you need to act like a responsible parent: repeat this rinsing and draining ceremony three or four times a day. You're aiming to keep the crop full of moisture to prevent it drying out.

7   It's up to you as to when you think your sprouts are ready to be eaten. We harvest after the beans or lentils have grown about 1cm (½in) high, but alfalfa can be left to grow a little taller. Drain one last time before cooking, and be sure to pick out and discard any unsprouted beans. The whole project should take between two and four days – fast enough for even the most impatient home farmer.

Tips

○ Consume your sprouts within the first five days.

___

○ If your home is particularly humid, refresh the water more frequently.

___

○ Set a timer or alarm so you don't forget to rinse your bean sprouts each day.

___

○ Cleanliness is really important with this task, so make sure you're using freshy cleaned or sanitised apparatus.

Garlic

A crime scene: you reach for the garlic at home, only to discover the poor unfortunate soul has been left in the prison of your kitchen cupboard way too long, its pleading green shoots reaching out for salvation.

Instead of disposing of the evidence, you can use these little garlic sprouts to grow your own garlic greens. With a milder flavour than a garlic bulb and the freshness of a spring onion (scallion), garlic greens make a colourful topping or great addition to a stir-fry. We prefer to use them as a last-minute home-grown garnish. You can also blend cooked garlic greens in a food mixer with olive oil and salt to make a simple green garlic purée – this makes a wonderfully fresh addition to a roast dinner.

The green shoots won't taste great at first — you'll have to let them grow at least a finger's length before you harvest them. It should also be noted that growing garlic greens on a window ledge is a proven deterrent to vampires ...

Growing speed	Fast
Difficulty level	Easy
Position	Sunny
Temperature	Medium
Use	Edible
Container	Small

You will need

Small jam jar
Fresh water
Kitchen scissors

To regrow garlic

1   Peel the outer skin of your garlic cloves, then position them in a small jam jar so their green shoots are reaching up to the sky.

2   Add fresh, cool water to a depth of about 1cm (½in): just enough to submerge the bottoms of the cloves.

3   Place the jar on a sunny windowsill and be sure to change the water at least every other day to keep your crop fresh and to avoid stagnation and bacteria.

4   Once they are about 10cm (4in) tall, harvest your garlic greens with a pair of sharp kitchen scissors. If you harvest just half of the green stem, the clove will continue to grow and serve you time and time again.

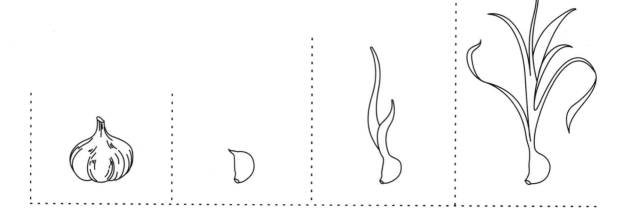

Regrown

Tips

○ Pick the largest cloves possible for regrowing.

○ Experiment with various varieties of garlic to see which you prefer.

○ If you let your garlic harvest overgrow, it will eventually flower. These little blooms make a perfect savoury garnish for the dirtiest of martinis.

Regrown

Mint

Mint is an excellent propagator. Many gardeners consider it invasive because it's so good at reproducing itself and can thrive in a wide variety of environments. In nature, mint tends to grow in very moist soils at the sides of streams, rivers and lakes, which means it's happily at home in a glass of water on your windowsill. It's these qualities that make mint such a fabulous contender for regrowing.

We love to grow mint on our allotment, partly because it's a fantastic herb to have on hand for cooking and cocktail-making, and partly because it's an environmentally friendly insecticide. As a companion plant, mint repels many unwanted insects. It can even be used indoors to kill common pests like wasps, hornets and cockroaches.

Last year we purchased a small camping stove that we keep in our allotment shed. There's an old stove-top kettle that we use to boil water if we're working outdoors on a chilly morning. We love to make our own mint and nettle tea, straight from the allotment, simply by mixing the leaves together in a mug, adding boiling water and letting the mixture steep for two or three minutes. The resulting hot drink is both warming and revitalising – give it a go.

Growing speed	Fast
Difficulty level	Easy
Position	Sunny
Temperature	Cool
Use	Edible
Container	Small

You will need

Sharp knife
Drinking glass or jam jar
Fresh water
Cultivation soil or potting compost
Small or medium-sized plant pot with drainage holes
and drip tray
Kitchen scissors

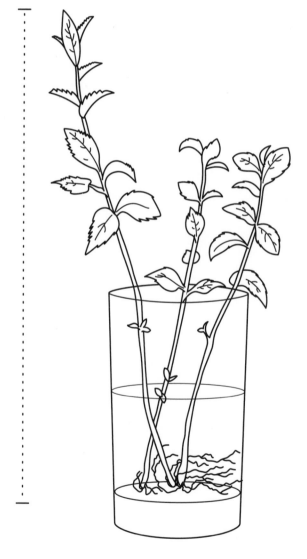

To regrow mint

1 Take a healthy stem of fresh mint and use a sharp knife to remove the lower leaves, leaving the bottom third of the stalk bare.

2 Place the mint in a jam jar or drinking glass and add enough cool, clean water to submerge the bottom third of the stem.

3 Position the vessel on a bright windowsill in a warm environment and be sure to change the water each day.

4 After around 10 days, your mint will have sprouted fresh new roots from the bottom of its stem. This means the cutting is ready to be transplanted into a plant pot or into the ground.

5 If you've chosen to grow your mint in a pot, it's a good idea to use cultivation soil, which is available from your local garden centre or online, but if you don't have any of this to hand, then regular potting compost can work well too. Take a small or medium plant pot and fill it with soil. Make sure your pot has drainage holes at the bottom and use a tray or saucer to catch any excess water if you plan to water the plant indoors.

6   Push the mint stems into the soil and gently compact the soil around them so that they stand up straight.

7   Water your plant pot regularly. Always remember that mint likes a damp environment.

8   You can place your fresh mint pot on a balcony, or anywhere in the garden. With a smaller pot, you could even try growing mint on your kitchen windowsill.

9   Harvest your mint with kitchen scissors as and when you need it. Once the plant's roots are well established to the ground and, providing you maintain its desired conditions, the mint will vigorously spring back to life.

Tips

○   Remember to trim away excess mint leaves on the stem so they don't make contact with the standing water.

○   Play around with some of the many varieties of mint, such as apple mint and water mint. Lavender mint and fresh strawberries make a perfect pairing.

○   Mint growing in a container can dry out easily. Water it daily in the summer months to keep the plant looking green and lush.

Regrown

Pak choi

(Bok Choy)

Pak choi or bok choy is a Chinese brassica. It has white or light green crunchy stems and wide green leaves. You'll find it in supermarkets, health food stores and farmers' markets in a variety of sizes from 5–30cm (2–12in) tall. All parts of pak choi are edible, but the most exciting thing about this vegetable is the rate at which it grows. The smaller varieties are ready to eat just 30 days after their seeds are sown. It's this speed and insatiable appetite that make this vegetable perfect for regrowing at home.

When you regrow pak choi at home, the results are almost instantaneous. Within the first few hours the plant will start to regrow itself. If you're keen to capture one of your regrowing projects with time-lapse photography on your device, then pak choi is the speedy little vegetable for you.

Any type of pak choi will work for the purpose of regrowing, but we recommend a larger 'true' pak choi variety over the smaller 'Shanghai' type, as the base of the plant is more robust and the finished regrown item is larger and more substantial.

Growing speed	Fast
Difficulty level	Easy
Position	Sunny
Temperature	Cool
Use	Edible
Container	Small

You will need

Sharp knife

Fresh water

Wide-necked jar or flat-bottomed bowl

Medium-sized plant pot with drainage holes and drip tray

Potting compost

Kitchen scissors

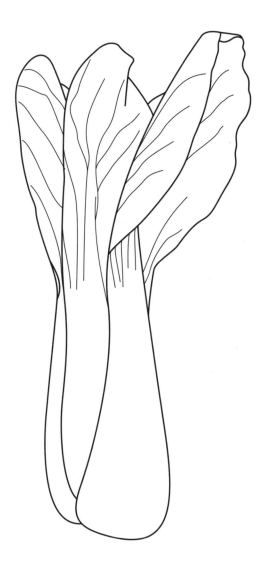

To regrow pak choi

1 As with many other projects in this book, the aim is to retain the lower part of the vegetable, where the roots are found, as this plays a vital role in bringing fresh water to the parts of your plants that need it most as it regrows. When you next use pak choi in the kitchen, use a sharp knife to slice through the stems, retaining the bottom 5–10cm (2–4in) of the vegetable.

2 Place the cutting in a wide-necked jar or flat-bottomed bowl and fill it with enough cool, clean water to submerge the bottom half of your cutting.

3 Position your vessel in a bright but cool location. You should see new growth appear in the first 24 hours, and within three days the cutting should be full of small new leaves and roots will be beginning to form. Be sure to change the water every day to keep it fresh.

4 After one week, inspect the cutting closely. If you've chosen to regrow the smaller Shanghai variety of pak choi you can harvest your crop as soon as you're happy there are enough new leaves for your purpose. Providing the water is kept fresh and clean, you can keep them growing in water for a couple more weeks before they lose their vitality.

5   If you've opted for the larger, original pak choi variety, you'll get more from your plant if it is now moved to a plant pot to continue its growth. After the first week in water, your cutting should have grown a number of small new roots underneath the waterline. If this is the case, you're ready for transplantation.

6   Take a medium-sized plant pot with drainage holes and an accompanying drip tray. Fill the pot with potting compost and create a small burrow in the middle of the soil, enough to accommodate your pak choi cutting. Place the cutting in the pot, ensuring all of the roots are surrounded by soil. Gently but firmly press the soil down around the plant.

7   Water the plant pot regularly, a little each day: enough to make sure the soil does not dry out but without over-watering. Place the pot in a bright, but cool location. This could be in a garden, on a balcony, or even indoors providing the temperature isn't too warm.

8   Harvesting is easy. Just use a clean pair of kitchen scissors to snip away the leaves as and when you need them. If you decided to plant your cutting in soil, providing the plant has a healthy root system, it should regrow time and time again, rewarding you with fresh crops of pak choi leaves through-out the year.

Tips

○ If you place your cutting in an overly warm environment of 25ºC (77ºF) or more, pak choi has a tendency to bolt. Bolting is when a plant is so stressed that it sends out a flower in a last-minute dash to procreate. A stressed brassica may look very pretty, and could reward you with a flush of yellow flowers. However a bolting vegetable loses its flavour and its leaves become bitter to taste.

○ As this plant comes from a warmer climate, don't be afraid of placing pak choi in sunlight.

○ The fast-growing pak choi is a great way to get children interested in gardening, cooking and healthy eating.

Regrown

Celery

If you're looking for a really easy, foolproof project to start your regrowing journey, then celery is a safe bet. In nature, celery grows in marshland, so it's inclined to grow well in wet environments. This means it springs to life quickly and robustly in a jar of water. To replicate its natural habitat, you'll have to keep your cutting moist while it grows.

You might associate celery with weight-loss diets. That's because it's become common knowledge that this plant provides you with fewer calories than you would normally burn during the time you eat it. So, this means if you ate nothing but celery for the rest of your life, you'd starve to death – albeit more slowly than if you ate nothing at all. On a cheerier note, celery plays an important role in Louisiana Creole cooking, and can improve the depth of flavour in a soup or stew.

Growing speed	Fast
Difficulty level	Easy
Position	Light
Temperature	Cool
Use	Edible
Container	Medium

You will need

Sharp knife
Wide-necked jar or flat-bottomed bowl
Fresh water
Spray bottle or mister
Kitchen scissors
Small plant pot with drainage holes and drip tray
Potting compost

To regrow celery

1   Using a sharp knife, trim off the bottom 8–10cm (3¼–4in) of a celery cluster. This means you're retaining the root-like area at the bottom of the plant. The inner heart of this section will regenerate into a refreshed celery plant.

2   Place your cutting in a wide-necked jar or medium-sized flat-bottomed bowl. Pour in enough fresh, cool water to submerge the base of the celery cutting, but do not add water to a depth of more than 4cm (1½in) at any one time, as too much water in the vessel can lead to your cutting becoming rotten.

3   Celery needs to be in a cool area to regrow, but it also needs bright, indirect light. A windowsill in a cool, bright room that doesn't get direct sunlight would be ideal. Use a spray bottle or mister to spritz the plant with water, daily.

4   Make sure you refresh the water every day, as this is the type of plant that quickly deteriorates in stagnant water. If you fail to keep the water fresh and clean, it will begin to smell and your celery plant will look pretty miserable. If any of your stalks become brown and slimy because they are in contact with the water, it's okay to snap or trim them off so that you're left with a fresh and healthy-looking cutting.

5   You'll notice the centre of the celery cutting beginning to grow in the first couple of days. The inner layers of stalks will grow in height and a beautiful fresh celery stem will start to tower above the rest of the cutting.

6   You can harvest your new celery leaves and stalks directly from your jar or bowl with a pair of kitchen scissors. However, if you're keen to let your celery grow even further, you must transfer the cutting to a medium-sized pot filled with potting compost. Be sure to choose a pot that has adequate drainage. Place the celery cutting into the pot and add a little more compost over the top to cover up your original cutting. Make sure you water your celery plant regularly so the soil remains damp but not soaking wet.

Tips

○ If you choose to grow celery outside, add plenty of compost and mulch around the plant to retain moisture.

○ Celery makes an excellent low-carb side dish for a hot meal. Simply sauté chopped celery in a hot pan with butter, salt and pepper. Add a little vegetable stock and a few chilli flakes (hot red pepper flakes).

○ You don't actually need to harvest celery right away. Try letting it grow for three months for a thicker celery stalk.

Regrown

Medium-speed growers

Regrown

Lettuce

When we started regrowing our own cuttings, we couldn't believe we'd spent so many years discarding living plants that were crying out to be given another chance at life. When you become familiar with the process, a fast-growing leafy vegetable like a lettuce will never look the same. The very part you might toss into your garbage or compost (the tough heart at the base) is packed with the powerful energy needed to regrow itself into a fine leafy specimen all over again.

Within the first few days regrown lettuce hearts begin to bubble with tiny new leaves, and within a few weeks the tender new stems of your future salad will be bursting into life.

Growing speed	Medium
Difficulty level	Medium
Position	Sunny
Temperature	Cool
Use	Edible
Container	Medium

You will need

Sharp knife

Jam jar, flat-bottomed bowl or plastic tray with raised sides

Fresh water

Plant pot with drainage holes and drip tray (optional)

Potting compost (optional)

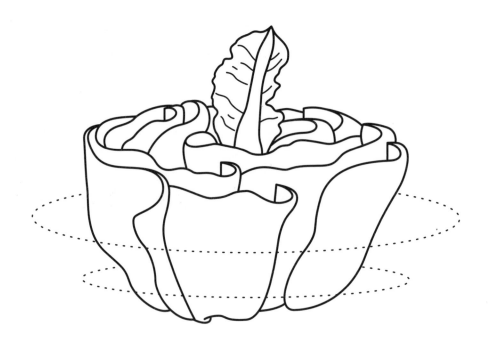

To regrow lettuce

1   When you're preparing a fresh lettuce to be eaten, make sure you cut off and save the bottom 5–7.5cm (2–3in) of the core. This section will now become your vegetable's lifeline to reincarnation.

2   Place the heart of your lettuce in a clean jam jar. If you are planning on regrowing more than one lettuce at a time, choose a shallow, flat-bottomed serving bowl or a plastic tray with raised sides so that each of your lettuce hearts can access the same amount of water.

3   Fill your vessel with enough fresh, cool water to cover the base of your lettuce heart, but not enough to submerge the top of the cutting. This is usually a depth of about 2–4cm (¾–1½in).

4   Place in a sunny location. It's recommended that you refresh the water every other day. This will avoid the water becoming stagnant, and will also replenish any liquid lost to evaporation.

5 Although new growth is on the way, you might see areas of the old lettuce heart that have become brown and withered. Carefully trim these away with a sharp knife so they don't contaminate your plant's water supply.

6 The fresh green leaves are ready to be eaten at any time, so it's up to you to decide how big you want them to grow before you snip them off and add them to your salad.

7 If you wish, you can easily transplant your growing lettuce heart into a pot of potting compost, which will give it enough nutrients to achieve a full regrowth.

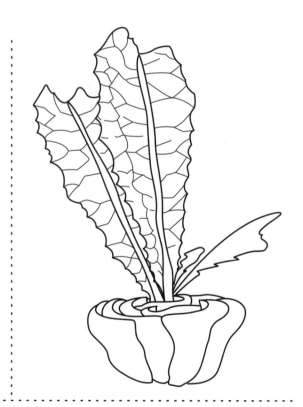

Tips

○   Trim away any brown leaves to avoid rot.

○   Tiny new leaves make a pretty garnish for hors d'oeuvres.

○   You'll always find new varieties of lettuce to experiment with. Try growing several different types together at the same time.

○   Grow lettuce on your windowsills all year round. With the right care and attention, you'll always have a homegrown salad on hand.

Beetroot

(Beets)

The rich purple-pink stain of beetroot (beet) juice is startling, even if you've been cooking with them for years. There's something ancient about their earthy taste — and if you eat too many, your urine turns pink!

They say beetroots were originally cultivated only for their greens, but by the time the Ancient Romans came along, their roots were on the menu too. There's a history of beetroot being used medicinally (often in relation to blood conditions) and we know its crimson has been used to colour all sorts of things, including human hair during the Victorian era.

When it comes to regrowing your beetroot, it's all about sprouting fresh leaves and stalks, both of which can be used in a variety of dishes throughout the year. For example, the greens make a wonderful side dish when seasoned, sautéed in butter and mixed with a little cream and roasted pine nuts. Before you start, it's good to know that the fresher your beetroot, the greater the yield for regrowth. We're lucky enough to have our own crop from the allotment, but many supermarkets and health stores sell fresh beetroot, particularly when it's in season.

Growing speed	Medium
Difficulty level	Easy
Position	Sunny
Temperature	Cool
Use	Edible
Container	Medium

You will need

Sharp knife

Medium-sized glass mason jar

Fresh water

Potting compost (optional)

Plant pot with drainage holes and drip tray (optional)

To regrow beetroot

1 Using a sharp knife, remove the top 3cm (1¼in) of the beetroot and retain this to regrow your greens.

2 If the beetroot top already has leaves coming out of it, cut these off and discard.

3 Place the beetroot top (with the leaves facing upwards) in a glass mason jar and fill with enough fresh, cool water to cover the base of the severed root by about 1cm (½in). You'll see the water turn a beautiful shade of pink, which will look gorgeous on a sunny windowsill.

4 The beetroot now needs lots of light to grow fresh leaves again. Place your jar somewhere sunny and bright. You'll notice the smallest flecks of bright green, baby beetroot leaves growing from your cutting within the first 24 hours, which is pretty remarkable.

5 It's important to refresh the water every other day, or daily in warm weather.

6   You can harvest the new leaves and stalks as soon as you see fit. We prefer to have several regrowing beets on the go at any one time so we can harvest a few of the leaves from each plant, rather than risk shocking the crop by removing all the leaves and stalks in one go. Eventually, the tops will stop producing entirely. At that point they are destined for the compost bin, but you might be surprised at just how much extra produce you garnered from such a small scrap of root.

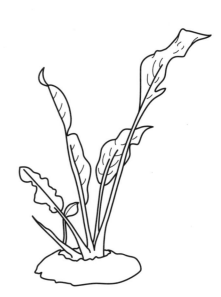

Tips

○ Try using a Blankoma variety. Its white root produces strong, tall tops which can be used like spinach.

○ Mix golden and red beetroots with carrots, purple radishes and other colourful vegetables for a technicolour rainbow salad you can be proud of.

○ Try using a plastic inbox tray to regrow ten or more beetroot tops at once.

Regrown

Fennel

If you have been lucky enough to take holidays in the Mediterranean region, you might have noticed wild fennel growing in its natural habitat at the sides of country lanes. Its yellow flowers and feather-like leaves make it distinctive once you know what to look for. The plant's characteristic anise scent might even give you flashbacks to sambuca shots on the dance floor.

Fennel has been used as food and medicine for generations. The British Library holds a 10th-century manuscript of the 'Nine Herbs Charm', a recipe for a potion used to combat the effects of infections in Anglo-Saxon England. It includes a poem that was chanted during the preparation of this remedy. Sweet-smelling fennel is one of the nine herbs used in the charm.

Fennel is a wonderful choice to regrow at home, not least because it looks so interesting as it grows. The plant's leaves are first to reappear from a fennel cutting, and these can be snipped off at any point and used in the kitchen. You could use your newly regrown fennel plants in a delicious cooked fennel, cannellini bean and blue cheese summer salad.

Growing speed	Medium
Difficulty level	Medium
Position	Sunny/indirect
Temperature	Medium
Use	Edible
Container	Medium

You will need

Sharp knife
Toothpick or skewers
Wide-necked glass
Fresh water
Kitchen scissors
Potting compost (optional)
Plant pot with drainage holes and drip tray (optional)

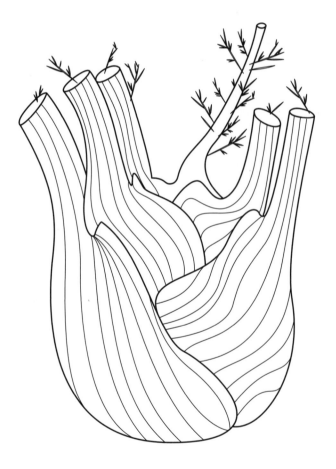

To regrow fennel

1   When you use fennel in the kitchen, be sure to slice off the root section and retain it, along with about 5cm (2in) of the adjoining bulb itself.

2   It's important that the majority of the fennel bulb remains dry when you regrow it. Take three toothpicks and position them equally around the circumference of your bulb, about 1cm (½in) from the top of the cutting itself, pushing them into the bulb.

3   Position your cutting (root area downwards) over the top of a wide-brimmed glass. A pint glass or beaker would work well. The toothpicks should rest on the rim of the glass, acting as a brace to hold the cutting in place.

4   Fill the glass with just enough cool, clean water to submerge only the root of your cutting. The rest of the bulb should be above water.

5 Place the glass on a bright windowsill, but not one that gets too much direct sunlight.

6 Remember to refresh the water at least every other day to keep your cutting clean and healthy.

7 Within days you will see small fennel shoots and leaves appearing from the cutting. Let these grow to your desired length before trimming with scissors and using when cooking.

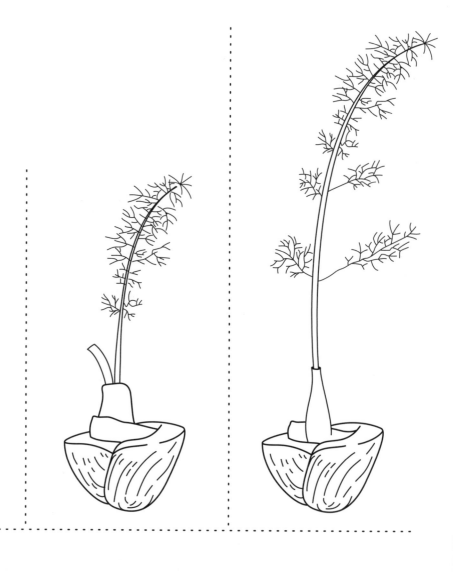

Tips

○ If your fennel starts to dry out, try spraying it with fresh water to increase humidity levels.

○ The tiny feathery leaves of fennel can be used when making pesto to add freshness.

○ Serve baked fennel with gorgonzola cheese, or use it to make a flavour-packed clam and fennel risotto.

Leeks

Many might know that the leek is the national floral emblem of Wales. When designing the coronation gown of Queen Elizabeth II, couturier Norman Hartnell asked if he could exchange the image of the Welsh leek for a daintier daffodil. Happily, his request was denied and the mighty leek took its rightful place on the Queen's ceremonial robes.

Leeks are surprisingly large when you see them growing in the soil on an allotment or on a farm. By the time they have reached your supermarket, they've often been trimmed into a neat pole shape, but out in the field, their leaves are long and splendid, like the trails of an exploding firework.

Growing leeks at home is a great idea, not just because they are fast-growing, but because the size and shape makes them an impressive and unusual houseplant.

And you really can't beat warm buttered leeks flavoured with thyme.

Growing speed	Medium
Difficulty level	Medium
Position	Sunny/indirect
Temperature	Medium
Use	Edible/ornamental
Container	Large

You will need

Sharp knife
Wide-necked drinking glass
Fresh water
Medium-sized plant pot with drainage holes and drip tray
Potting compost
Kitchen Scissors (optional)

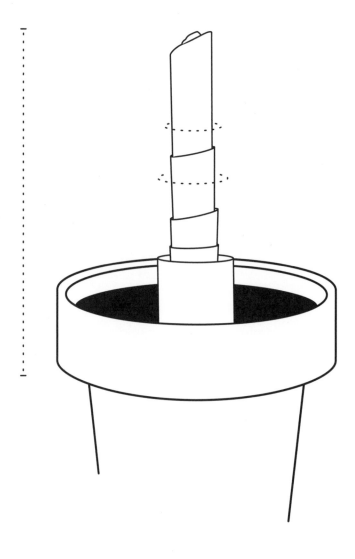

To regrow leeks

1 The next time you buy leeks at the supermarket, make sure that you select specimens with a good amount of healthy roots at the base. When you come to use your leek for cooking, use a sharp knife to cut off and retain the bottom 8cm (3¼in) of the vegetable. This will be the foundation of your new leek plant.

2 Place the cutting in a glass of room-temperature water. The water should cover the roots of the cutting only.

3 Place the glass on a bright windowsill, but out of direct sunlight. Change the water every other day to prevent the leeks from becoming slimy or producing an oniony odour.

4 Leave the leeks in this position for the first two weeks. After a few days, you'll notice that the roots themselves have been growing stronger and longer.

5 Now the leek is ready to be transferred to a plant pot filled with potting compost. Make a small furrow in the soil, just enough to cover the base of the leek plant where the roots have formed. Gently press down the soil around the stem so the leek is standing upright, and add a little more potting compost if needed. Place your plant pot in a bright, but cool location – a balcony would work well, but we have regrown leeks in the living room to great success.

6   Keep the soil moist by watering daily, but be careful not to over-water. Within a few weeks, you'll be rewarded with fresh green leaves, and over time, your leek will grow tall and strong, and look more like a piece of ornamental bamboo than the little cutting you started off with.

7   You can harvest your leek at any time by slicing off parts of the stem using a sharp knife or a pair of kitchen scissors. Providing the plant is kept watered and has access to light, you will be supplied with fresh leek cuttings time and time again.

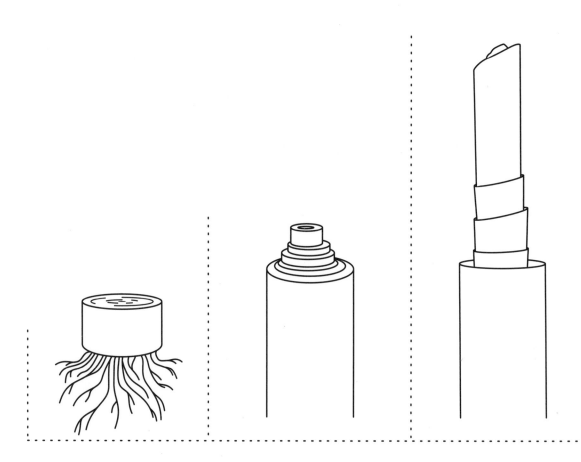

Tips

○ A quick 'cheat' is to simply place your freshly bought leeks in a vase filled with water. The leeks will start to grow right away.

○ If you change the water in a jar of leeks every day, you can avoid an oniony scent in your living room.

○ Try leaving leeks to grow tall and flower rather than eating them. The result is truly majestic (page 14).

Coriander

(Cilantro)

The famous TV personality and cooking teacher Julia Child once said that her advice on dealing with coriander (cilantro) was to 'pick it out and throw it on the floor'. Not everybody loves the taste of coriander, but those that do appreciate this herb for its fresh, citrusy punch that is one of its defining characteristics dishes across the world, be they from Mexico, the Mediterranean or Thailand.

Scientists now believe that coriander-haters have a variation in a group of receptor genes that allows them to perceive something called aldehydes. To this unfortunate group of people, the herb tastes like soap. Personally, we absolutely love coriander. Its lemon-and-lime flavour turns a squashed avocado into guacamole, and coriander seeds are key to perfecting the flavour of many wonderful curries and stews.

It's difficult to grow coriander from a rootless stem, so next time you're shopping for the herb, be sure to purchase a bunch of coriander that still has parts of its roots attached. These are more common in health food shops and Asian grocery stores.

Growing speed	Medium
Difficulty level	Medium
Position	Sunny
Temperature	Warm
Use	Edible
Container	Small

You will need

Sharp knife
Drinking glass
Fresh water
Small plant pot with drainage holes and drip tray
Potting compost
Kitchen scissors

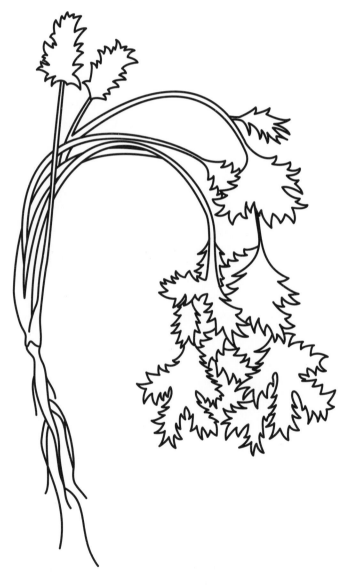

To regrow coriander

1   Select a good-sized handful of coriander stems with the roots intact.

2   Use a sharp knife to remove the bottom 5cm (2in) of the stems. Retain these for regrowing and use the delicious leafy tops as you wish. Be sure the stems have a visible root – if this is not present, the following steps may not work.

3   Place your root cuttings in a small, clean glass and fill it with just enough cool water to cover the root section.

4   Place the glass of coriander cuttings somewhere bright and warm be sure to change the water every day. Within a couple of days, you should notice that the coriander stalks are beginning to grow and produce tiny new coriander leaves. This is a great sign that you're on your way to reproducing a new, healthy coriander plant.

5   When you're confident that the roots have begun to regrow, too, it's time to transfer the coriander to a plant pot so it can continue to prosper, nourished by the various minerals that are found in soil.

6 Place the roots in the hole and add more potting compost if necessary, gently compacting the soil around your coriander.

7 Put a suitably sized drip tray or saucer underneath the plant pot to prevent spillage, and water your coriander plant thoroughly. Coriander prefers fairly moist soil, so allow excess water to pool in the saucer below. If your plant starts to dry out, it will draw up liquid from the base.

8 Place the plant pot in a bright and sheltered position (this can be indoors or outdoors). Water the plant daily, paying close attention to the moisture of the soil and making sure the plant isn't too dry.

9 Within weeks, you should be rewarded with a healthy, bushy crop of coriander. When you come to harvest the herb, use a clean pair of scissors to take what you need, but leave at least one leaf on each stem so that the plant remains healthy and in a good place to grow back once more and serve you again in the future.

Tips

○ Coriander plants don't usually need feeding, but an occasional liquid feed of balanced fertiliser can act as a quick pick-me-up.

○ Check with your guests before you serve them coriander. They might think it tastes like washing-up liquid.

○ Keep trimming back and harvesting coriander, and you'll be compensated with more growth.

Regrown

Carrots

During World War II, a rumour began to circulate that carrots could make you see in the dark, and in the UK, the Ministry of Information supposedly made a link between successful RAF fighter pilots and their carrot consumption. This idea seemed to stick with the British public. Whether it remains a genuine belief or just an excuse to encourage children to eat their vegetables is one of the great unanswered questions of our time.

Regrowing carrots is a fairly simple process, but before you imagine serving up your own regrown carrot cake, it's important to know that when you regrow carrots, it's actually for their leafy greens. Over the years, carrot greens have built up a bad reputation, with some sources even suggesting they're inedible. This isn't the case, and a quick online search shows an abundance of interesting carrot green recipes and ways to reinvent these highly nutritious, vitamin-packed leaves.

This system only works with carrots that still have some of their leaves attached at the top, or at least a brown stump where the leaves should be, so bear this in mind when you're carrot shopping.

Growing speed	Medium
Difficulty level	Easy
Position	Sunny/indirect
Temperature	Cool
Use	Edible
Container	Medium

You will need

Sharp knife

Medium-sized glass mason jar or flat-bottomed serving bowl/tray

Fresh water

Medium-sized plant pot with drainage holes and drip tray

Potting compost

Kitchen scissors

To regrow carrots

1   The next time you use carrots in the kitchen, retain the top 5cm (2in) of the carrot and cut off any carrot greens (be sure to use these in a recipe, providing they are fresh and healthy).

2   Place your carrot cuttings with the top facing upwards in a medium-sized jar or flat-bottomed serving bowl. To ensure a good yield, it's best to regrow a few carrots at once, so you might choose to use a small plastic tray — it will need to have raised edges that can contain water.

3   Fill the container with enough cold clean water to almost cover all of the orange carrot root, but be sure not to submerge any of the area at the top of the carrot which will produce your green shoots.

4   Place the container on a sunny windowsill or in partial sun and be sure to replace the water daily.

5   Within the first few days, carrot greens should begin to re-emerge from the top of your carrot cuttings. At this point, it's time to transfer your growing vegetables to the soil.

6   Fill a medium-sized plant pot with potting compost and position your carrot tops with the green ends coming up out of the soil. About 2cm (¾in) of your 5-cm (2-in) cuttings should be visible and protruding from the soil.

7 Keep watering your pot of carrots in order to keep the soil moist. How frequently you need to water will depend on the temperature and humidity of the environment, but try not to over-water your plants or they may begin to rot.

8 You can grow your carrots indoors or outdoors, on a windowsill, on a balcony, or even plant them directly into the ground in the garden or allotment (as we do).

9 The carrot greens become tougher the longer you let them grow, so we advise harvesting your greens while they are still young. To harvest, simply snip off the leaves with a sharp pair of scissors and rinse them before using them to cook.

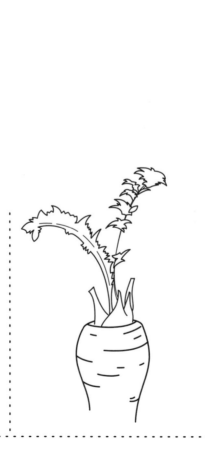

Tips

○ Don't be afraid to ask your greengrocer when they will be receiving a fresh delivery of produce. The fresher your original vegetable, the greater its chances are at healthy regrowing.

○ We enjoy eating freshly chopped carrot greens in dishes like tabbouleh as a parsley substitute (they're part of the same family), but the greens are also brilliant — just wilt in the pan.

○ Use them as you might use spinach in any number of cooked dishes, such as a carrot-green cannelloni or a wilted carrot-green Welsh rarebit.

Regrown

Lemongrass

Last summer, one of our allotment neighbours maintained a beehive. This was wonderful, as it meant that the crops on our patch acted like a giant food hall of free nectar for thousands of insatiable bees. Needless to say, we had a perfectly pollinated crop and a fantastic harvest. Sadly, this spring we learned the beehive was empty. The bees had left, absconded.

Perhaps if we'd had access to some lemongrass oil, we could have tempted the bees back into their hive. In bee-keeping, lemongrass imitates the pheromone emitted by the glands of the honeybee to attract bees to the hive. However, a more common use for lemongrass is in Thai cooking, where its wonderful, fragrant citrus taste flavours stir-fries, curries and marinades.

Fresh lemongrass should feel heavy in your hand, full of oil and moisture. Much of the lemongrass sold in supermarkets has begun to dry out, and while it may retain its citrusy flavour and be suitable for home cooking, we recommend you use the freshest lemongrass possible if you're planning to regrow the plant.

Growing speed	Medium
Difficulty level	Medium
Position	Light
Temperature	Warm
Use	Edible/ornamental
Container	Small/medium

You will need

Sharp knife
Fresh water
Drinking glass or jam jar
Small or medium-sized plant pot with drainage holes
and drip tray
Potting compost
Kitchen scissors

To regrow lemongrass

1   Use a sharp knife to slice through your lemongrass stalks, retaining only the bottom 8cm (3¼in) of the stem. This should be the most bulbous part of the lemongrass and is lighter in colour than the rest of the stem.

2   Take a clean drinking glass or jam jar, choose the size depending on the number of lemongrass plants you're aiming to regrow. Place the lemongrass cuttings in the vessel with the bulbous end at the bottom. Fill the glass or jar with cool, clean water, but be sure to only submerge the lower half of the bulbous area. It is in this zone that the new roots will soon grow.

3   Place your vessel on a bright windowsill or anywhere that is both warm and full of light.

4   Change the water every day to keep it fresh, while keeping an eye on your cuttings for signs of regrowth. These should appear within the first 14 days. You should soon see a cluster of roots growing from the bottom of your cutting.

5   When you're absolutely sure your lemongrass has begun to regrow, it's time to transfer it to a plant pot so it can begin its journey to becoming a fully grown lemongrass plant once more. Take a small or medium-sized plant pot with adequate drainage and fill it with potting compost.

6 Transfer your lemongrass cuttings directly into the potted soil, submerging the base of the cutting into the soil up to around half the height of the bulbous area. Thoroughly water your plant(s) and place the pot in a bright, warm location. Remember to keep watering your new plant(s) so that the soil doesn't dry out.

7 Within a matter of weeks, your lemongrass will grow in height and strength. To reap your harvest, use a sharp pair of kitchen scissors to cut into the living plant, but be sure to only remove the top half of the shoots so that your plant can continue to grow.

8 Lemongrass plants look really great as house or garden plants, so bear in mind you don't necessarily have to eat them to feel totally satisfied with your growing project.

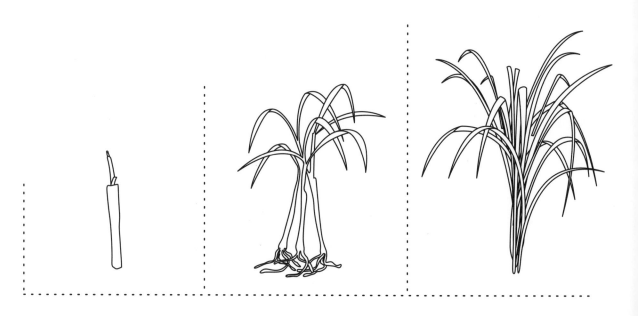

Tips

○ To make a lemongrass gin and tonic, take one or two stem cuttings of your regrown lemongrass, bash them using a pestle and mortar and add them to a 250ml (8½fl oz) bottle of gin along with the peel of a fresh lime. Leave to infuse overnight. Use the lemongrass-infused gin as you would in any gin and tonic. The infusion adds a wonderful aromatic quality to the cocktail.

○ Potted homegrown lemongrass makes a great house-warming gift.

○ Lemongrass is also known as citronella. In warm climates where it grows wild, the plant forms huge tufts of tall grass up to 2m (6½ft) in height. If you live in a part of the world that experiences a cold winter and plan to grow lemongrass for ornamental purposes in your garden, it's a good idea to plant the lemongrass in a pot so it can be brought inside to a garage or porch over colder months, to avoid being damaged by frost.

Slow growers

Regrown

Mushrooms

When you begin your mushroom regrowing journey, you probably already know that something magical lies ahead. Mushrooms and toadstools have long been associated with fairies, the supernatural and psychedelic trips. Fungi are neither animal nor vegetable, and when you come across them growing in their natural habitats, it's easy to understand how they have worked their way into folklore.

In the wild, mushroom spores only reproduce new fungi when they haphazardly land in the perfect spot. Similarly, we have to create the perfect environment in terms of temperature, darkness and moisture to allow the mushroom stems to regrow. Usually, spores develop into mycelium (a fur-like fine fuzz). You should be able to see this furry material on any fresh mushroom stem, and it is this magical matter that will reproduce a new mushroom harvest.

There are a number of options available when it comes to growing media for this project, including coconut fibre, used coffee grounds, soil or manure. It's advisable to do a little research to find out the best medium for the type of mushroom you want to grow. For our example, we chose to use hay to regrow oyster mushrooms. Available in small quantities from pet shops, hay is sweet-smelling and more appropriate for your kitchen cupboard than horse manure.

Growing speed	Slow
Difficulty level	Difficult
Position	Dark
Temperature	Medium
Use	Edible
Container	Large

You will need

Sharp knife

Shoe box or cardboard box (preferably with a lid)

Small bag of hay

Spray bottle or mister

Cling film (plastic wrap) or a plastic bin bag and sticky tape
(if your box doesn't have a lid)

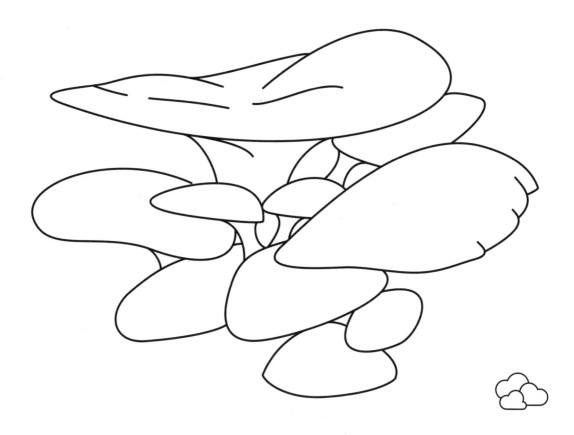

To regrow mushrooms

1   Next time you're cooking with mushrooms, remember to retain the stems. Using a sharp knife, chop the stems into 1-cm (½-in) chunks and set them aside.

2   Take a shoe box or cardboard box and spread a 2-cm (¾-in) layer of damp hay across the base of the box. The hay will act as the medium in which your mushrooms will grow.

3   You can further moisten your layer of hay by spraying it with water from a spray bottle. You want to ensure that it is damp but not completely wet.

4   Next, add a layer of chopped mushroom stems, dispersing evenly across the bed of hay.

5   Now apply another layer of damp hay and give it another spritz of water.

6   Mushrooms grow in the dark, so if you're growing these in a shoe box, put the lid on and pierce several holes in the top to provide ventilation for the medium and mycelium below. If you don't have a lid for your box, cut out a suitable piece of cling film (plastic wrap) or plastic bin bag and tape this to the top of your box, remembering to add some holes for ventilation.

7   Place your box in a dark environment with a temperature of about 18–24°C (65–75°F). Return to the box each day to give it a light spritz of water, ensuring that the hay remains moist but never completely sodden nor completely dry.

8   After about two weeks, you should see the fine fuzz of the mycelium starting to develop on the hay. Two or three weeks later, your mushrooms will be ready to harvest.

Tips

○ Oyster mushrooms love to grow on dead trees, so consider adding a small log to your mushroom-growing box.

○ Enrich mushrooms with Vitamin D by placing them in the sun before you eat them.

○ Fresh mushrooms are short-lived, but you can always make them last longer by drying them out in an oven on a very low heat and storing them in a clean airtight jar.

Regrown

Avocados

When we were growing up in the 1980s, avocados were always called avocado pears. Imagine the disappointment of biting into its fatty flesh and expecting to taste a juicy, ripe fruit! Over recent years, the avocado has become massively popular. It's beautiful contrasting colours of black skin and green flesh and its adaptability in a whole range of dishes have made it the subject of many an Instagram post.

Botanically speaking, the avocado is really a large berry with one giant seed inside. It appears to have originated in central Mexico, where it has been cultivated for hundreds of years. The modern name 'avocado' actually comes from the old Aztec term ahuacati, which means 'testicle'. We think this makes this curious-looking knobbly-skinned treat all the more intriguing.

You can grow an avocado plant from the stone (pit). It's unlikely that the plant that follows will fruit, but it makes for a beautiful ornamental curiosity, and the growing process itself looks fascinating. If you are aiming to grow your own avocados, you need to wait around 15 years for your avocado plant to turn into a fully-grown tree — and even then, you would have to cross-pollinate with another adult plant. This sounds like a bit too much work for us, but if you're feeling ambitious, don't let us stop you.

Growing speed	Slow
Difficulty level	Difficult
Position	Sunny/indirect
Temperature	Medium
Use	Ornamental
Container	Medium

You will need

Sharp knife
Paper towel or clean dish cloth
Toothpicks or skewers
Wide-necked drinking glass or jam jar
Fresh water
Pan scrub or scouring pad (optional)
Medium-sized plant pot with drainage holes and drip tray
Potting compost

To regrow avocados

1   When you remove the stone (pit) from your avocado, do it carefully and try not to slice too far into the surface of the stone. Rinse it under cool running water and use a piece of paper towel or a clean dishcloth to remove any flesh still sticking to the seed.

2   You'll notice that the stone isn't completely spherical; it's more like an egg shape. Identify the pointy end of the stone and make sure that this point remains facing upwards throughout all the subsequent steps. Using the edge of a knife, gently peel away the outer skin of the seed to reveal the seed's inner skin (this should be pale, like the colour of a cashew nut).

3   Take three toothpicks or skewers and push them carefully into the stone, about halfway down the egg shape and evenly spaced around the circumference. You only need to pierce the stone with the tips of the toothpicks.

4   Take your new seed structure and place it over a wide-brimmed glass or jam jar. The toothpicks will act as a form of scaffolding, suspending your stone in the glass or jar. Now fill the vessel with cool clean water, just enough to cover about half of the avocado stone. Immediately place your glass or jar in a sunny area – a bright windowsill would be ideal.

5   You'll need to change the water every day to keep the seed fresh. If you see the inside of the glass has become green or discoloured, it's a good idea to clean it out to prevent the water becoming stagnant. If the submerged part of your stone starts to look blackened, don't worry. Your plant is still perfectly healthy – it's just the stone reacting with the water below. If you don't like how this looks, it's perfectly okay to use a pan scrub or scouring pad to gently remove the dark patches, but take care not to damage the tender new roots when you do so.

6   Now you must exercise a little patience, as it can take over a month for the stone to split open, descend roots and begin its transformation into a small avocado plant. Alien-like tentacles will fill the glass, and elegant, slender leaves will shoot from a growing stem.

7   When the stem of the plant is around 20cm (8in) tall, it's time to transplant your avocado sapling into a plant pot. Take a 20-cm (8-in) wide plant pot with drainage holes at the base and fill it to just under the brim with potting compost.

8   Carefully remove the toothpicks from your avocado stone and transplant your seedling into the pot by burrowing a small hole with your fingers. The hole needs to be big enough to accommodate the roots and allow for the stone to be completely covered by the surrounding soil.

9   Keep your new houseplant in a bright location and water it regularly. Place a saucer or drip tray underneath your plant pot.

Tips

○   We've always had good luck when growing our avocado stones, but many people struggle and recommend growing multiple stones at once in case the seed fails to germinate.

○   Colourful vintage cocktail sticks add a whole new dimension to the look of your growing seed, so play around with different styles.

○   Consider using a hyacinth forcing vase for a clean, modern look.

Pineapples

Pineapples are extremely sensitive to cold. When they were first imported from the tropics to temperate Europe, they were rare enough to be the envy of even the wealthiest of households. In the 18th century, King Louis XV of France was presented with a precious pineapple grown at Versailles, and Russia's Catherine the Great ate pineapples grown on her own estates at huge expense. So great was their status that the pineapple's primary role was to decorate dinner tables in the stateliest of homes. Pineapples were often used time and time again to impress party guests before eventually rotting away.

As a warm and sunny climate is critical for the pineapple to fruit, this may not be achieved at home when you're growing from a cutting (depending on where in the world you live). However, the plant itself is great to look at, and — if you're lucky — after a few years, you may see a small pineapple fruit pop its head up from the foliage.

Pineapples may have travelled many miles before they reach your supermarket shelves. By the time the fruit is fully ripe and ready to eat, the leaves at the top may have become browned and dry. It's important to use a good-quality fresh pineapple with the greenest of leaves for the purpose of regrowing, so bear this in mind when you're shopping for the fruit.

Growing speed	Slow
Difficulty level	Difficult
Position	Sunny
Temperature	Warm
Use	Edible/ornamental
Container	Medium

You will need

Sharp knife
Toothpicks or skewers
Jam jar
Fresh water
Medium-sized plant pot with drainage holes and drip tray
Potting compost

To regrow pineapples

1   Cut off the top part of the pineapple. You are aiming to retain the leafy bit at the top and a small section immediately below that will form the core of the new plant. Trim away any fruit around this section and remove one or two of the smaller lower leaves that were closest to the fruit itself.

2   Take three toothpicks or skewers and insert them evenly around the newly trimmed pineapple stem, roughly where the lower leaves were positioned. This will form a structure to suspend the pineapple stem over the water, without getting the leaves of the pineapple plant wet.

3   Take a medium-sized jar and place your pineapple stem structure over the jar, filling it with cool, clean water so that the lower part of the stem is submerged in water and the leaves remain dry.

4   Place your jar on a sunny windowsill in a warm location. Brightness and humidity are extremely important for your plant to regenerate.

5   After about seven days, you should see several small roots becoming visible at the bottom of the cutting. At this point, transfer your cutting to a medium-sized plant pot filled with potting compost. Be sure to use a pot with drainage holes at the bottom, so as not to drown your new pineapple plant.

6 Keep your potted pineapple plant in a sunny and warm location and water it regularly, just enough for the soil to remain slightly moist (as pineapples grow in humid tropical locations).

7 Over the next few weeks, you will notice the leaves at the top of your cutting becoming longer and broader. Over time, your pineapple plant will grow large — and, if you're lucky, one fine day a baby pineapple will emerge from the centre of the plant.

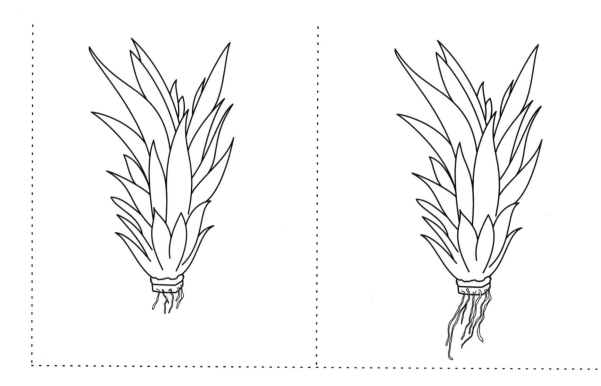

Tips

○ Regrowing pineapples can be difficult. In preparation for this book, we made four attempts before our pineapple cutting began to grow roots. Remain patient – it's worth having another go if you fail.

○ Readers living in a tropical climate might have better luck with this project.

○ When serving fresh pineapple, add a little salt to make it taste sweeter.

Regrown

Tomatoes

Most people know that tomatoes are actually a fruit: a type of berry, in fact. Perhaps you associate tomatoes with Italy, but the truth is they originated in South and Central America and didn't find their way to Europe until the 16th century. It's astonishing to think of all those Ancient Romans lazing around feasting, and not one pomodoro in sight.

Heirloom tomatoes are the best choice for regrowing from seed. They come with a range of brilliant names, such as Banana Legs, Big Rainbow, Hawaiian Pineapple, Lollipop and Yellow Pear. Unlike the seeds of hybridised plants, heirloom seeds 'breed true'. This means collecting seeds from a ripened fruit and using them to grow a new plant will reward you with all the characteristics of the original.

Regrowing tomatoes from seed requires quite a lot of space, as they can grow up to 2m (6½ft). They are best suited to a greenhouse (glasshouse) or a space outdoors, such as a balcony or patio. If you have the space, you can absolutely grow them indoors – they love the conditions of a sunny windowsill, and having the plant right under your nose means you're more likely to give it the daily watering it requires.

Growing speed	Slow
Difficulty level	Medium
Position	Sunny
Temperature	Warm
Use	Edible
Container	Large

You will need

Sharp knife

Jam jar

Fresh water and a sunny spot

Sieve (strainer)

Paper towels

Potting compost

Plastic seeding tray

Large plant pot with drainage holes and drip tray

Ruler and pencil

Water spray bottle or mister

To regrow tomatoes

1   Using a sharp knife, cut your ripe heirloom tomato in half and scoop out the inner part of the tomato, along with its seeds.

2   Place the seeds and flesh in a jam jar and add about the same volume of water to the jar. Seal the jar and shake up the contents.

3   Place the jar anywhere in your home. The contents of the jar will start to gently ferment over the course of one week. Give the jar a gentle shake each day, and at the end of the week, you should see your seeds have separated from the rest of the mix and have sunk to the bottom of the jar. This process of decomposition is important, because it helps fight against the transmission of diseases to the seeds.

4   On the seventh day, open the jar and fish out your seeds. Place the seeds in a sieve (strainer) and rinse with water.

5   Now place your tomato seeds on clean paper towels and leave them to dry out for one week. After this, your tomato seeds will be ready for the next step – planting.

6   Fill your tray to the rim with potting compost. Pick up the tray and give it a tap to make sure the soil has found its way to the bottom of each cell, and add more on top if necessary.

7 Use a pencil to make a 1-cm (¾-in) burrow in the centre of each of the cells. Carefully take your tomato seeds one by one and drop them into your prepared planting holes. Add a little more soil on top to cover the seeds.

8 Using a watering can or spray bottle dampen each of the cells so that the soil is moist.

9 Some seeding trays come with a plastic cover or dome – if this is the case with yours, apply it now. If not, or if you're growing your seeds in small pots or containers, take a piece of cling film (plastic wrap) and secure it over the top of your container. The aim is to create a warm and humid environment to help your seeds come to life.

10 Place your tray in a bright and warm position and keep an eye on the soil to make sure it stays moist (but not wet) over the coming days. Ideally, your tray should receive around eight hours of direct sunlight daily, so the summer months are ideal timing.

11 This is the moment you've been waiting for. Within 7–14 days, you should see signs that your seeds have germinated and perfect little tomato seedlings are raising their heads in the dark soil. Remove the plastic or lid. You can leave the seedlings to grow in their cells until they have grown two or three sets of leaves, at which point each seedling should be carefully transferred to its own larger plant pot.

12 Before your let your plants spend the night outside in the cold, it's advisable to 'harden them off' by introducing them slowly to a cooler environment over the course of a week. Simply take your seedlings outside for a few hours and bring them back inside, increasing the hours spent outside daily. Eventually, they will be accustomed to the temperature.

Tips

○ When your tomato plants start to grow, be sure to 'pinch out' the side shoots. This is new growth that emerges in the axil between the stem and the leaf.

○ In their native habitat, tomato plants are perennials, meaning they automatically return each year and bear fruit. Cultivated tomatoes are annuals – the tomato plant completely dies away each year, so gardeners across the world grow their crop from seed early in the spring for a summer harvest.

○ Tomatoes are greedy when it comes to water. Satiate their thirst with consistent and abundant watering.

Ginger

Ginger has such an evocative flavour. It was one of the first spices to be traded in ancient history, and its distinctive taste and smell can be reminiscent of many different worlds, from the vibrant aroma of Thai restaurants through to the scent of a gingerbread house at Christmas.

Ginger grows best outside in tropical and subtropical climates, so if you're regrowing it at home, it's best to imagine it as a houseplant (or a balcony or patio plant that comes inside over winter). Its tall, grassy leaves give it an interesting look, and if you're as desperate for attention as us, there's nothing more impressive than offering your guest a cup of ginger tea and then uprooting a plant in your living room to get hold of the freshest ginger root possible.

If you examine a piece of root ginger, you'll see it's covered in small bumps or sprouts. If you've ever neglected to use ginger in time and let it grow old in your kitchen cupboard, you've probably noticed these bumps turn into fresh green shoots. If you want to make multiple ginger plants from your ginger root, you'll need to make sure that every piece of ginger you plant has one of these small bumps present.

Growing speed	Slow
Difficulty level	Medium
Position	Sunny
Temperature	Warm
Use	Edible/ornamental
Container	Large

You will need

Sharp knife

Large plant pot with drainage holes and drip tray

Potting compost or 'sterile potting compost' (see page 17)

Fresh water

To regrow ginger

1   To grow multiple ginger roots, take your rhizome and use a sharp knife to cut it into several thumb-sized pieces (be sure that each piece contains its own bump). Let your ginger pieces dry in the open air for 24 hours before you proceed to the next step – this is to ensure the ginger isn't vulnerable to infection. If you are planning to grow one large ginger plant, it's okay to just use a whole piece of ginger root, without cutting it up.

2   Fill a large plant pot with fresh sterile potting compost. Submerge your ginger roots under the soil with the bumps facing upwards, about 4cm (1½in) below the surface. If you are planting multiple ginger pieces in the same pot, plant them 10cm (4in) apart.

3   Water the pot so that the soil is damp but not completely sodden. Use a drip tray under your plant pot to catch any excess water.

4   Place the plant in a bright and warm location and continue to water it so that the plant doesn't entirely dry out. Now it's a waiting game. After several weeks, you should see new green shoots emerging from the soil. A few months later and your ginger plant should be full of greenery and brand-new stems and leaves. Below the surface of the soil, the rhizomes should be growing in size too.

5   To harvest the ginger, simply break away part of the living root for use in the kitchen. When the plant reaches a good size, you can start the whole process over by digging up the ginger root, but retaining a few pieces for the purpose of regrowing.

Tips

○   Ginger root skin is perfectly safe to eat, so for most recipes there really is no reason to bother peeling it.

○   As a ginger plant grows in soil, it will require larger quantities of water. Keep an eye on the lushness of the leaves and the dryness of the soil to make sure the plant isn't getting too thirsty.

○   Ginger leaves are edible too. Add them to couscous or chop finely to add a fragrant twist to tabbouleh.

Regrown

Potatoes

Potatoes are one of the most rewarding crops grown on our allotment. They are fairly easy to grow when you follow a few simple steps and their crop is usually bountiful. When harvest time comes and you begin to dig them up, the gleaming new potatoes shine in the rich, dark soil. A patch of earth has become a goldmine. It's an exhilarating feeling, running your fingers through the dark soil to retrieve another, then another, until you're satisfied you've salvaged the lot. One small potato can generate up to 20 new tubers.

The process of regrowing your potatoes is simple. However, you first need to decide whether you're going to grow your potatoes in a pot, a grow bag or directly into the earth. The benefit of using a form of container is that it minimises the amount of digging required at harvest time. Potatoes aren't the right type of plant to grow on your windowsill or kitchen countertop. The leafy part that appears above the soil grows up to 1m (39in) in height, so bear this in mind before you begin your potato-growing journey.

We also recommend you use organic potatoes for this process. Some supermarket-bought potatoes have been treated to stop them sprouting too soon in your kitchen cupboards, and this would work against you if you have plans to regrow your spuds.

Finally, it's worth noting that most potatoes will grow best if planted in the spring.

Growing speed	Slow
Difficulty level	Easy
Position	Outdoors
Temperature	Cool
Use	Edible
Container	Large

You will need

Sanitized sharp knife
Plastic tray
Large bucket, plant pot or fabric growing container, with
drainage holes (optional)
Garden soil
Compost mix
Garden fork (optional, if growing in the ground)

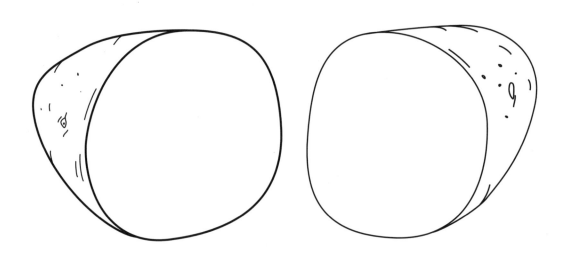

To regrow potatoes

1

Make sure that your potatoes are ready to be regrown. A quick look at any potato and you'll see small dark spots. These are the potato's 'eyes' and each one has the ability to sprout. Using a sharp, freshly sanitised knife, cut your potato into two or three evenly sized sections, making sure that each one has its own 'eye'.

2

The exposed interior of the potato is often susceptible to bacterial infections, so you now need to dry your cut potatoes in the open air until their inside flesh has become dry to the touch. Leave the potato pieces on a tray in a cool environment until the eyes begin to sprout – this process is called chitting. Don't worry if your potato pieces start to look sad and shrivelled – it's important that they've reached this stage before they are submerged in earth.

3

If you're planting your potatoes in a bucket, pot or grow bag, fill the container with a 50/50 mix of compost and garden soil. Leave a gap of a couple of centimetres (an inch) at the top of the pot so that it doesn't overflow when you add your potato pieces. Position your potato pieces 10cm (4in) under the earth and about 20cm (8in) apart. Depending on the size of your container, this might mean you're only growing one or two potato plants in the same pot or bag, but that one container could go on to produce a great deal of potatoes.

4 If you're planting directly into the earth, it's a good idea to dig trenches, again about 10cm (4in) deep, and position the potatoes with the eye facing upwards at 20-cm (8-in) intervals. Cover the potato pieces with soil.

5 When your potato pieces are covered with soil, it's time to give them their first watering. The soil should have a similar feel to a damp sponge – wet but not sodden.

6 Water your potato plants regularly. This could be daily if you're choosing to use pots or grow bags. Plants growing directly in the ground requires less watering, but it's still important to regularly monitor your crop and attend to the plants' needs as necessary. If your potato plants produce small green fruits resembling a cherry tomato, don't be tempted to eat them. They contain the toxin solanine, which is poisonous to humans.

7 Your potatoes will be ready to harvest when the plant has flowered and wilted – this can take between 70 and 120 days, depending on the variety of potato. When the plant above ground looks dead, it's time to dig down and recover your potato hoard. If you've grown your potatoes in a pot or bag, simply upturn the container, but if you've chosen to grow directly into the earth, use a garden fork to gently lift the soil, working through the earth with your hands so you don't miss any smaller potatoes.

8 If you've grown a number of potato plants, you needn't harvest them all on the same day. Your potatoes will keep perfectly well under the ground for weeks — or even several months — before they start to sprout again themselves.

Tips

○ If you're serious about growing potatoes, it's wise to purchase 'seed potatoes' for planting. These will produce a greater yield than a supermarket potato, which is essentially grown only to be consumed.

○ When your potato shoots first emerge from the ground, mound more soil on top, covering the plant. This is known as 'earthing up', and will encourage more potatoes to grow.

○ Potatoes benefit from a nitrogenous fertiliser.

Regrown

Onions

You probably paid for this book with a debit card, a credit card, or perhaps in cash, but in the Middle Ages you might have paid your way with a home-grown onion. Onions were so valuable and sought after that many people paid their rent in onions. That probably wouldn't go down well today, but that doesn't mean the world has fallen out of love with this special vegetable.

When you regrow an onion, you are really doing it for the green onion sprouts (green stems that emerge as the onion regrows). Green onion shoots make a great alternative to spring onions and work well in stir-fries and as a flavoursome addition to a fresh salad.

You can use a fresh onion for this project, or if there are older sprouting onions in your kitchen scraps, these are perfect too. It's so sad to think of how many perfectly healthy onions are thrown away every day when they could so easily be repurposed and regrown at home.

Growing speed	Slow
Difficulty level	Medium
Position	Sunny
Temperature	Cool
Use	Edible
Container	Large

You will need

Sharp knife
Shallow dish or saucer
Fresh water
Large plant pot with drainage holes and drip tray
Potting compost
Kitchen scissors

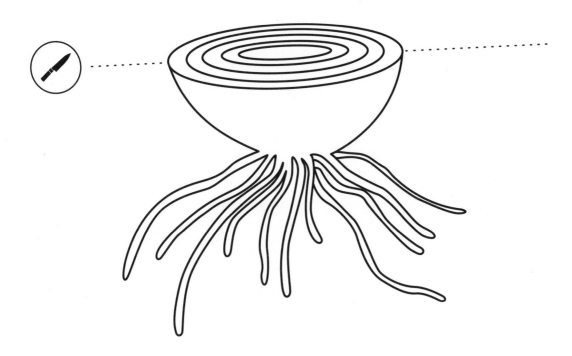

To regrow onions

1   The next time you use an onion in the kitchen, be sure to retain part of its base, as this is the area from which it grows roots. You'll need at least 3cm (1¼in) of the bottom part of the onion for this project.

2   To encourage the onion to grow roots, place it in a shallow dish or saucer with the base facing downwards and add enough cool, clean water to cover the base of the onion. Change the water daily for the first few days and keep an eye out for new root growth.

3   Once you are sure that your onion cutting is growing healthy new roots, and you can see that fresh green shoots have started to reach upwards from the centre of the cutting, it's time to transfer your onion into the earth so it can continue to grow.

4   Fill a large plant pot with potting compost and create a hollow or indent large enough to hold your onion cutting in the centre of the pot. Position the cutting in the hollow and use a little more potting compost to cover the older part of the onion. Your fresh onion shoots should now look nice and neat in a bed of soil, with no sight of your original onion trimming.

5   From this point onwards, you need to keep your potted onion plants in moist soil, so remember to water it regularly. You can choose to plant your onion cutting directly into a raised bed or directly into earth in your garden. If you do this, you won't need to water it as regularly, but as with all plants, it's best to monitor it and tend to it accordingly.

6   When the fresh onion shoots are 10–20cm (4–8in) high, you can use a clean pair of kitchen scissors to trim them off for use in your kitchen.

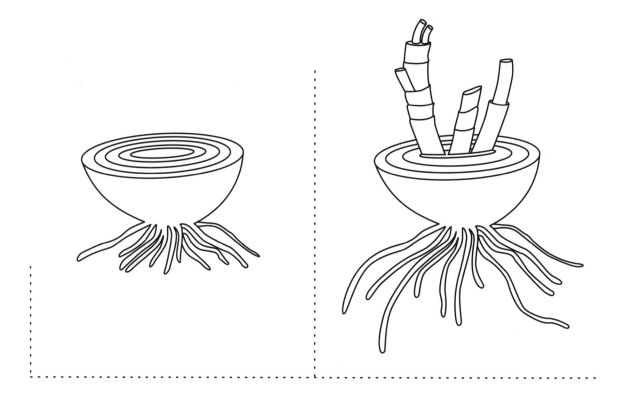

Tips

○ Onion juice can make head hair grow faster if you apply it to the roots. Just remember to wash your hair before you hit the disco.

○ If you come across an old overgrown onion which has already begun to sprout, simply remove the skin and outer onion layers until you reach the green centre. You'll have a ready-made onion plant ready for planting.

○ You can use onion skins to dye fabric if you're so inclined.

Index

About the authors

Two Dirty Boys

Paul and Robin met randomly on a dark Halloween night in 2010 and have haunted each other's lives ever since. Together they run Two Dirty Boys, a Instagram blog about their allotment plot in Bow, East London. Unafraid of making mistakes and always willing to give something a go they enjoy sharing their successes and failures with friends and followers. Together they grow ingredients to make pickles, pies, teas, wines and cocktails. Awe-struck by nature they take great delight in the joys of germination, propagation, and fermentation.

Follow them @twodirtyboys

Paul Anderton

Paul grew up in Lytham St Anne's, Lancashire, the son of two teachers. His interest in natural curiosities started in his childhood with his collection of exotic pets and reptiles. He first attempted to regrow a pineapple cutting with his father when he was nine years old.

He holds a degree in English Literature & Theatre Studies from Lancaster University and a Masters in Arts & Cultural Management from St Mary's University of Minnesota, USA, and now runs a London based brand partnerships agency named Bicycle. His home is Bethnal Green where he lives with hundreds of houseplants and his beloved border terrier, Willy.

Robin Daly

Born in Devon and raised on the cream of her rolling hills, Robin first started gardening with his grandmother, spending hours pottering about her seaside greenhouse. She instilled her love of the natural world and the wonder of growing your own food. Robin left his Devonian idyll for the bright lights and smoke of London to Study Molecular Genetics at Queen Mary, University of London.

He kept up his love of gardening, moving his pots between rentals before settling in Stoke Newington and finally getting an allotment – after 7 years on the waiting list! Robin is a BAFTA winning TV producer and lives with his black and white cat, Leo.

Acknowledgements

To Kate and Munir for the opportunity.
To Eve for her patience.
To Paul's dad and Robin's grandma for the inspiration.